# BEYOND WORDS

ARNAB SARMA

India | USA | UK

Presentation by *BookLeaf Publishing*

Web: www.bookleafpub.com

E-mail: info@bookleafpub.com

ISBN: 9789363303294

First edition 2024

*'BEYOND WORDS' is dedicated to my family members expressing my feelings and emotions which I could have never expressed in front of them directly.*


*I believe my family members and especially my Dad will be so proud to see me publishing my debut poetry book and continuing his legacy as an Author.*

# ACKNOWLEDGEMENT

I want to thank my Late Father-in-Law, Shri PULEN CHANDRA GOGOI who after passing away showed up in my dreams and requested me to write a book and make my family members feel proud through it.

So, in due respect to his heavenly soul, I started writing this poetry book with full dedication.

I really thank once again my Late Father-in-Law for believing in me to be like my dad who is also an author and an academician.

# PREFACE

*Beyond Words* is a collection of my untold words or unexpressed feelings and emotions towards my family members in the form of poetry.

I may live or be gone tomorrow but my love and memories will be alive through this book. The words of gratitude that I will never be able to say or express has got the place in this book through poetry.

# If I Hadn't Met You

If I hadn't met you, I would have never known,
What true love is all about.
I would have never felt this secured,
Nor would I have changed for the better.

If I hadn't met you, I would never have,
The pleasure of love and romance.
I would have missed the bliss and the craziness,
That love brings with its silly dance.

I feel your smooth touch,
I long to hear your sweet voice.
As no other could take the place,
You are the only one, I have no choice.

If I hadn't met you, I would have never changed,
Nor would I have known what to do.
I would have been searching for my other half,
Left incomplete, if I hadn't met you.

# Love Is the Answer

Our love is the answer,
We have been together for quite a while.
I love you for so many things,
Your touch, your presence, and especially your
smile.

With you, there's nothing to hide,
I'm drawn to you in total trust.
You're irresistible to me,
And I give myself willingly to you.

Your devotion feels so sweet,
And I pounder my heart for you.
You love me no matter what,
And I'll always love you like I do.

# My Most Wonderful Girl

You're my most special one,
Your smile shines as bright as the sun.
You're so smart and caring,
For you, my heart truly sings.

I'm happy that I have chosen you,
You are the best among the rest.
You are my cute little pearl,
I love you, my most wonderful girl.

# Your Love Is A Magical Gift

When I think of you,
You fill my heart with an emotional touch.
I've never had such thoughts before,
I'm lost in you, my love for life.

Your love is a magical gift,
A wonderful miracle and my greatest treasure.
Your love creates in me,
A sense of peace, ecstasy and bliss.

Your love gives me,
A feeling of safety and stability.
You are the best thing,
That ever happened to me.

# Until I Found You

Before I met you, my love,
I thought I was so happy.
But I had never known,
The deep satisfaction and total fulfillment,
That you have brought.

When you came into my life,
I felt a lot of things.
But had never experienced,
This blissful feeling.

You made me look deep within myself,
To find the fresh new in me.
I thought I knew about love,
But I didn't, not until I found you.

# One Special Person

We're facing life together,
We're handling each joy and sorrow.
I'm so glad that you are by my side,
Let whatever may come tomorrow.

I never thought that,
I will spend each precious minute,
With just one special person,
And that's you, where I find happiness within.

You're my perfect partner,
A sweet lover and a trusted friend.
You are safe in my love,
The love that will never end.

I've learned so much from you,
About giving, sharing, and loving.
Now I know if I hadn't met you,
I wouldn't have really been living.

# With You Forever

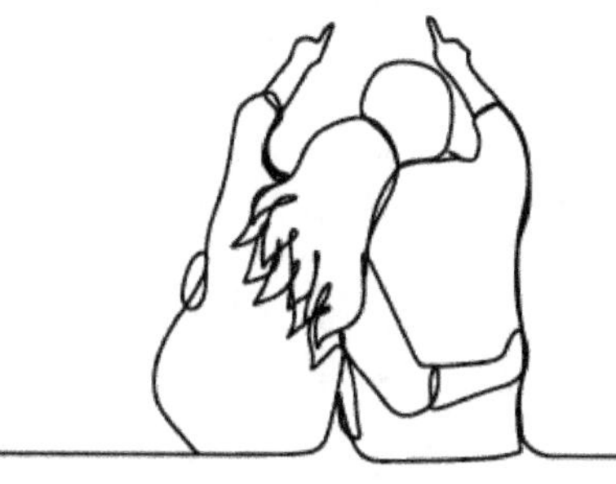

You're my sweet, wonderful wife,
And that's what you'll always be.
I can hardly believe the good fortune,
That has been blessed upon me.

You fill my life with pleasure,
You're my very own treasure.
Without you, I'd be empty inside,
Let's cherish the good times together.

Each year spent is a blessings from you,
And that's sure and certainly true.
Each year binds us stronger and deeper,
And I wish to be with you forever and ever.

# Bliss

Of everything that I love and treasure,
In you, I find my perfect pleasure.
I love the way you spend time with me,
These memories will never disappear.

I love your touch and the way you kiss,
To be with you is pure heavenly bliss.
Of everything that I love and care,
I find in you my perfect pleasure.

# Holding Your Hands

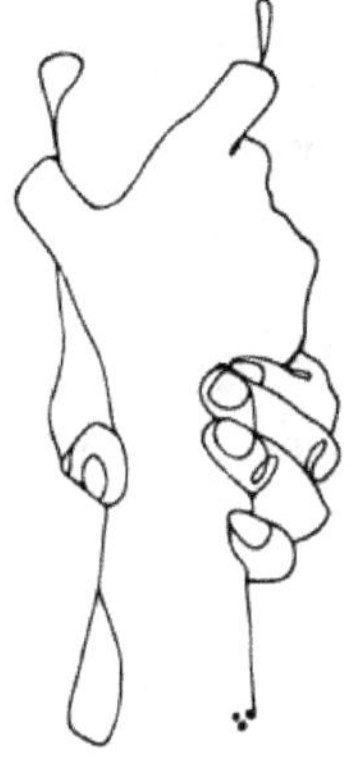

When I hold your hands,
It warms my heart and soul.
It's hard to imagine,
How I could love you more.

Just looking at your face,
Gives me so much thrill.
I love you now,
And I always will.

# I Never Knew

I never knew such happiness,
I didn't think that dreams would come true.
I couldn't really believe in true love,
Until I finally met you.

Every day is thrilling with you,
And all my dreams really came true.
You belong in my arms,
And I'm totally hypnotized by your charm.

# In My Dreams

In my dreams a long time ago,
I imagined my true love;
A perfect match and my soulmate,
Who will be an angel from above.

You're here now,
And now I know.
Our love will stay and thrive,
And together we will make it grow.

# Life Shine

I'm thinking of you,
All day and night.
You're deep in my heart,
And I keep you by my side.

Oh, love of my life,
I'm so glad you're mine.
I want you forever,
To make my life shine.

# Love Time

If I had all the time in the world,
I know what I would do.
I would have spent every moment,
In pleasure, by being with you.

You make my heart sing out of love,
You know how much I care for you.
Spending the rest of my life with you,
Now I know why I have you.

# My Everything

When all goes wrong,
And my life gets stuck.
I think of you every time,
And my life gets unstuck.

In the midst of chaos,
You make my heart sing.
You're my peace and happiness,
You're my truest everything.

# Rocked My World

Dear, when you touch me,
It fills me with bliss.
My whole world is shaken,
Each time we kiss.

With everything you say and do,
I fall more deeply in love with you.
My whole world is rocked,
Each time I hug you.

# If Tomorrow

If tomorrow my life ends,
With many things left to do.
It won't matter at all,
Because I had lived with you.

I will be in your fond memory,
For the years to come and go.
I had lived with you, my dear,
That will be my heavenly blessing.

# God Sent Blessing

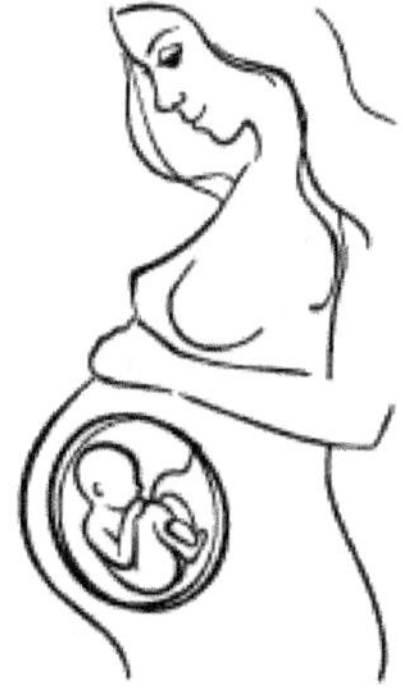

Baby, you are a Godsend blessing,
That makes our lives worthwhile for living.
You complete us and give us a purpose,
You manage to make us smile even when you
are crying.

When you gently clasp our fingers,
Or as we gaze down at your little feet,
We remind ourselves each and every day,
How precious they are, so special and sweet.

We hope you will be respectful and humble,
With a life filled with happiness and peace.
God bless you, my little angel,
Have a life as colorful as the rainbow.

# A Gift for Life

Your cute little eyes and nose,
Your cute little cheeks and sweet smile,
Your adorable babbling,
Will be lovingly treasured forever.

Your cute little hands and feet,
Your little walk and the mischiefs,
Your cheerful embrace,
Will forever be a gift for life.

I hold you against my chest,
The place you love and sleep the best.
I can feel the rhythm of your breathing,
It's a little moment filled with so much meaning.

# Our Little Miracle

Our baby changed all things,
That will never be the same.
Our life is filled with wonder,
Since our little miracle came.

There's so much to be done,
But the time is short and slips quickly away.
Our family gains more love,
And the bond will never erase.

Seeing her tiny fingers,
And her bright eyes on her face.
Taking our time for all the good,
That comes along with these parenthood days.

# Memories We Will Always Treasure

We're so glad that you joined our family,
Yet you make us wonder.
A little miracle package like you,
Has a voice as loud as thunder.

You are so small and cute,
For whatever you want,
You just open your mouth,
And cry like nobody is with you.

You're a gift more precious than diamond or
gold,
You are a brand-new baby to love and hold.
Holding onto each baby pleasure,
For the memories we'll always treasure.

# My Guiding Angel

From the time I was really young,
I realized I had someone,
Who always cared and protected me,
Yes, that's you, my mom.

You taught me right from wrong,
And guided me towards the right path.
You took care of me in every possible way,
You have been my constant guiding light.

My heart is filled with love for you,
I found my guiding angel and a friend in you.
You are my teacher and also my caretaker,
You are my mother who makes my life simpler
and better.

# Your Love Is A Mystery

Mom, your love is such a mystery,
How can you do it all?
You're always there with a solution,
For all my problems, whether big or small.

Your love protects me every day,
I feel safe and sound.
I can do anything confidently,
Whenever you're around.

Mom, your love is such a mystery,
I can't understand it at all.
You love me no matter what,
I'm glad that I can feel it all.

# Wisest Mom

I wish I could tell you,
How much you mean to me.
I'm the person that I am today,
Because you let me be.

Your love, so unconditional,
Makes me happy, secure, and strong.
Your examples in your teachings,
Has made me confident and mature.

There is no other person,
Better than my mother.
You are the wisest person,
That I have ever known.

# Thank You Mom

Mom, you express your love for me,
In so many different ways that can be.
You make me feel so important,
With all your praises and encouragement.

You're always there when I need you,
To comfort me and to care.
I know I may trouble you all the time,
But your love follows me wrapped in my arms.

Thank you, Mom, for all you've done,
And for giving me all your time.
I love you from the bottom of my heart,
You're a Godsend blessing of mine.

# A Secret Good Friend

I'm admiring you today, Dad,
You're the strength of your home.
You're the person to seek for advice,
Who can do anything with perfection.

I look up to you with respect,
More than words can convey.
I love you, Dad, and I'm so blessed,
For you're my father and the very best.

You're smart and you're strong,
Just a perfect Dad-blend.
You're my father and my adviser,
And a secret good friend.

# Loving Super Dad

I can always count on you,
You're the wind beneath my wings.
You are the rock and the foundation,
Where our life begins.

Dad, you can do anything,
You're smart as smart can be.
I wish to walk holding your hands,
But that's a secret wish which I couldn't fulfill.

There's so much more about you my dad,
That I would like to say.
But now I'll just end up saying to you,
That you're my loving super dad.

# Secret Superhero

You are my secure foundation,
You are my secret superhero.
I'm filled with fond appreciation,
Every time I think of you.

You make me feel protected,
Though I never said it to you.
You were always there for me,
Whenever I needed you.

You have a place of honor,
Deep within my mind and heart.
You are always my secret superhero,
Though I never said it to you.

# Beloved Mother-In-Law

Thank you for being such a wonderful mother,
For raising your beautiful daughter.
Thank you for being supportive and helpful,
For letting me marry your wonderful daughter.

You always trusted us,
And never interfered in our lives.
You're always so warm and loving,
As years passed, I found a second mother in you.

You've embraced me with love, right from the
start,
A mother-in-law like you is an amazing work of
art.
A poem for you to show how much I care,
Dear mother-in-law, you are a true gem.

# Beloved Late Father-In-Law

I got a new father,
The day I married your daughter.
That feeling made me happy,
And also left me a little bit in awe.

You were a man who cared for everyone,
With deep understanding and a golden heart,
You were filled with so much wisdom,
No wonder that's why my wife is such a
diamond.

You were so cordial to me,
Thanks, you welcomed me into your family.
Though you are not with us now,
A part of you will always remain within me.

# Gone Beyond the Sky

(A Special Dedication to my Late
Father-in-Law)

With love, warmth, and words untold,
Your memory fills our soul.
Though you're gone beyond the sky now,
Your spirit stays by us all.

You taught the life's most precious thing,
To your daughter, and now my wife,
Faith, courage and how a soul takes wing.
Your every words of wisdom,
Will be treasured by us, though you are gone.

Though we can't hold your hands again,
Nor sit with you like we used to,
Yet you will live within our beating heart,
And we'll never be apart from you.

Someday we'll all meet beyond the sky,
And all the earthly longing will fall apart.
Until then, we have your presence,
And memories in our beating heart.

It won't be easy to live up to your ideals,
It won't be easy to see mother-in-law without
you.
It won't be easy to look at you,
Through photos and videos.

But we will make it through,
We will survive, just like you wanted us to.

9 789363 303294